I0485482

The
SPEEDChange™
PROJECT

The Paradigm that Transforms Teams Without Training

Mubeena Mohammed

ISBN-13: 978-1516810024   ISBN-10: 1516810023

Table of Contents

A Poetic Disclaimer

I wrote this book in a 3-week spree. Like everything I write, the book wrote me. In some places I say "he" and in some I say "she", only to keep continuity. To the trainers, managers and powers at be if you don't agree, take what I say lightly. To the Agents of Change who believe like me, let's join forces immediately.

Foreword

By Roland Sullivan, Editor of Practicing Organization Development Series (Wiley, 2014)

By the grace of God, I am one of the original ˉ00 change agents in the National Training Labs and Kurt Lewin tradition. Such are the frontrunners of the existing change and transform world that is the current rave. Therefore, I am proud to witness the new thinking presented in this book. Its philosophy and ideas are truly revolutionary for today's world, where change in organisations is the need of the hour. There are a couple of reasons I am testifying to the brilliance of this work.

In my last edition of *Practicing OD*, David Bradford (Stanford University) wrote in the Foreword about his concern regarding what he perceived as the diminishing role of OD. He said only a few are actually doing true OD. Others work in piecemeal projects, and they lack a sophisticated theory of change that truly works to transform the whole business.

Also, coming up in my Forth Edition, we compare OD with the current change management movement. Change management is focused on tools, and training on individual jobs. More is needed just at my long time professional colleague, Mubeena says in this exciting right on book.

With The **SPEED**Change™ Project, a deeper theory and execution of change is upon us. It addresses Bradford's concern that business results are not achieving breakthrough status because of too narrow a focus. It also sheds light on W. Warner Burke's (Columbia University) contention that training does not successfully create organisation-wide change.

Having worked with Mubeena since 2004 and known her personally for 10 years, I know of very few individuals with her depth of instinct and analysis. Let me self disclose. Both of us have degrees in Philosophy. This gives her stunning inputs into how individuals, teams, and organisations are evolving in the current milieu. Having lived in Dubai, India and the U.S. she has amazingly unique perspectives on organisational behavior and the human spirit.

Her presence and work in the Middle East is of paramount importance at this time. To the Middle East I say - Your potential is enormous. Seize it and shine. It is no wonder that her name Mubeena in Arabic means "self-evident; obvious; clearly manifested".

With the precepts in this book, she has sensitively adapted advanced models of change for organisations with conventional management styles. The **SPEED**Change™ Project will change the way organisations change, lead and transform for greater, faster and resistance-free results.

Her work is gaining ground as more businesses start to take note that training has not worked for them. They need better systems to get quicker, deeper, cost-effective results, where training and project management have royally failed to deliver. I am blown away with the simplicity and truths of the approach here, and thoroughly enjoy her personal, light and humorous writing style.

"2M" as I call her, is well on her way to becoming one of the world's most sought after thinkers and futurists. Her forecasts about future business practices eerily resonate with many Fortune 500 CEOs. Some of whom I know personally admit to me, 'That's exactly where we're going".

I particularly identify with her stance that organisations will be boundary-less in years to come, but I might not agree with her on one thing. She says this will not happen in her lifetime. I think it may well do with her at the helm, and a whole new momentum of parallel thinkers, in a place such as Dubai, the fastest changing city in the world. Why not learn from her right now. Come to the leading edge yourself.

Leaders looking for a method beyond training to grow and develop their people will be refreshed, humored and relieved with this book. It contains golden tenets that will rattle a few traditionalists but will also inspire a whole new cohort of Change Agents.

I am so excited to be part of the new wave that The **SPEED**Change™ Project is already creating. It is my absolute conviction that her methods will spawn a massive redirection for human capital.

The process in this book is the tipping point that will align teams and businesses like you've probably never seen. Soon enough, organisations, governments and entities will have to perfect this Project internally to stay viable and thriving. And I have no doubt about the natural inevitability of this, as our businesses continue to demand the bottom-line of what's better for them.

So enjoy. Reflect. Apply to your life. Start now. Be a leading edge change maker.

Roland Sullivan.

Preface by the Author

This book is not intended to be scientific undertaking. I do not cite any scholarly works and the reasons for this become apparent as you read it. I've personally written every word and all the ideas and client experiences I talk about are raw from the heart.

Not many business books come from the heart. Even though so many businessmen and women I speak to off the record tell me about how they make decisions with heart first and numbers second. This book is dedicated to those leaders who want to get to the heart of the matter.

I wrote this book on a whim with no planning and very little editing. As I say in my poetic disclaimer, the book wrote me. This little discourse came as a first response to clients who continue to pick my brain with the billion dollar question, "What's a better way for our team to learn and develop owing to the lack of ROI in training today?"

I've wondered why a better way for employees to learn and apply lessons back on the job hasn't arrived with all our modernity. I explore some explanations of this, drawing on the last 13 years of my work.

My educated guess is that many of the myths I expose here will resonate with you, whether you're an Employee, Manager, or

Owner. Instinctually there is a knowing that we need a better way to involve our people to grow and develop to serve our businesses.

Efforts to connect training and performance have eluded leaders and I offer a new connect. After designing The **SPEED**Change™ Project, I am testing it with clients raising concerns with ineffectiveness of training. Later editions to this book will include a compilation of case stories.

Many ask me what the model is. But every leader experiencing unique benefits is creating their own. No external model will do. For now, results so far have given me an inspired impetus to share the Project's principles.

Nominate your team to participate as a test group, and be part of the case study project at www. **SPEED***ChangeProject.com.*

Training is Passé

Take it from me, someone who has advised businesses on their people-related strategies for more than a decade. Training doesn't work. And I think we should re-think the whole idea of everything "training" – objectives, methodology, delivery, content, material, and most of all in my view, the redundant concept of a know-it-all trainer. Gasp! I heard you. Now relax and give what I have to say a listen because it already is a game-changer in my circle.

What is the first response when I ask leaders what their people need in order to learn, change and grow? "More training". But I have come to firmly believe that traditional training is irrelevant at best in the times we live in. And why?

Because the money spent on training is not realized well enough. Ask any of your potential high flyers about the effects of training on their performance. Their truthful answer: "It was fun, great hotel and amazing food... the trainer's suit and tie matched very well. But I don't know what I would do different at my job after this."

The story is all too familiar in organisations the world over – send people to training where an external expert stands on a pedestal and badgers down rigidly factual information to untrusting attendees, especially if they are the millennial kind, and all they end up getting is bored.

Then back they go into their toxic work environments where learning does not transfer onto the job. Traditional scuffles ensue where CFOs breathe down the neck of well-intending Human Resource Managers. They rightly ask, "How on earth was that training spend ever justified? Our people are more confused than ever with all these concepts flying around, but are now demanding more of these courses because they've found the most convenient way to get days off." If this scenario, or at least a version of it, does not happen in your company, I'd be very surprised.

We are far beyond the old ways of doing business where success was synonymous with a brick and mortar type company. Every single day I read about startups getting financed for millions without a single employee on board or a single office brick being laid. But why have most organisations still not adapted to moving away from the brick and mortar classroom style lecturing for their people? Oh! "We have e-learning and blended styles", you say? When was the last time you could accurately demonstrate to your CFO, or anyone, that learning really occurred, got applied, and produced significant change?

So why do I incessantly harp upon the idea that training does not work? Because business and people are going through a major shift right in front your eyes. From a "here are the systems, facts, and the absolute right way to do things" model to a "how are customers responding to our current processes, and what's the next wave for us, and who do we really want to be in all of this?" paradigm is begging for a new orientation when it comes to learning and development of talent.

You see, the truth is that most HR professionals, much like the education sector, haven't thought about another option to traditional lecture and blended teaching. Why? Because it's a safe card to play and organisations usually use this card as the poster child for their employer of choice, public relations, and branding strategy. "We develop our people" is still the most cited mantra around. But how is this exactly done?

No matter how many leaders try to convince mə they got somethin' different, I've never come across a "program" good enough to create ultra dramatic shifts in performance. Just doesn't happen. But "more training" is still considered the arswer! This is sadly nothing more than the automated Pavlovian response that leaders have fallen trap to.

Imagine a training provider coming into your organisation and offering an in-house or public sales training program. The sales pitch goes like this, "Our program has the best experts who've been doing this for the past 20 years in the region, delivering the latest techniques that guarantees results in 6 months. Your employees will get the skills they need to beat your competition and they will master the science of selling." Whoop dee doo. You buy the program and send your team to this course.

For two days, the expert instructs your team on how to use one technique after another. Oh but not before the expert explains the principles and core model behind the perfect sales strategy. This seems like a great place to start but it can be the most damaging in terms of true learning. Why do I say that? Because you are asking your team to re-wire core beliefs about what may be working positively for them.

The number 1 sin that training programs commit is the force-fitting of views and thoughts of people into alien models that aren't relevant for the culture or value system that their organisation purports to espouse. Most attendees of training courses complain to me in my qualitative interview work - that they are left overwhelmed and confused by experts who don't know their capabilities, and that they feel they are not good enough to achieve the ideals laid out in the program by the end of it.

"Plus, who is this trainer guy anyway? He doesn't know me or my customers and he comes in telling me what to do!" Over the years I've seen direct evidence through my client work that training is not sustainable and is only craved by those who want an escape from official routine. If that in itself is not a cry for help, what is?

More on What Training Does (Not)

We haven't quite moved on from the military roots of our modern HR industry. Employee testing and training are remnants of the alpha and beta tests used during the World Wars. Soldiers had to be quickly categorized into groups based on mental abilities. Very few realize that at the time, testing had to be done due to a lack of time and preparedness. Today, a lot of mass organisational training and testing is done believing it's a shortcut to efficiency. Not so.

Don't get me wrong. I'm not saying we should stop using instructional techniques with our military, or our salespeople for our bestselling products, or our doctors, or our commercial pilots, or anybody that needs to get to a certain level in order to perform core duties ethically and soundly. But using it for development does not go to the heart of the matter. The matter with our current paradigm of "instruct on the facts" is that the success story is left unfinished.

Our current story is "be the best you can be and training will get you there." Think out of the box? Why don't we just remove the box altogether! To be the best you can be will take more than instruction manuals. It will take inspired action. It will take application. It will take questioning the status quo. It will take self-doubt. And it will take emotion.

Why is training the go-to solution for businesses? Because most of these programs are nothing but robotic stimulus response exchanges that avoid the so-called pain of real change at the workplace.

It's all very well to say that all of this training should be thrown out the window. But HR Managers tell me constantly, "You got a better option?? Managing change in our company also relies on this very training!" Now this always makes me laugh. Especially when I get requests for "change management training" or "cultural integration training" or "trust training" or "corporate values training". Roll out the red carpet for the trainer!

Here's an all-time classic: "Can you deliver a one day training program on innovation for our top team of 20? It has to be one day because our leaders do not have the luxury of more time. By the way we require a 5-star venue with a menu to match. And your ground rules cannot bar the attendees from answering important business calls." The logic in investing in 8 hours for 20 smart people to be directed by someone who does not know them or their company on a list of factoids does not hold up.

For the record, here would be my answer to potential clients with similar requests: "Sir/Mam, the million dollar advice I can give you for free is to log on to Google or Amazon, search for books and content on your subject of interest, and direct your team to the search results. Voila, you've just become a world-class expert! Please do not hire our company to simply regurgitate the techniques and principles of innovation, when the information is out there at the tip of your fingers." The average 7 year old can source information better than you and I today.

I respectfully remind well-intending leaders all the time that their people are not Pavlov's dogs. In my humble experience, training does nothing more than this - classically conditions employees on every organisational process so that an alternate or new response is automatically rejected by virtue of the prevailing drumbeat.

So here's sin number 2 of structured training programs. Content writers and trainers claim to have inside knowledge that is privileged. Training providers have somehow persuaded team leaders and others that Google and Amazon are not enough to gain access to their privileged information. Schools teach our kids how to leverage Google. So why not iTunes University, TED Talks, Udemy or Coursera for employees? And for crying out loud, why aren't organisations harnessing the power of their own expertise internally? Where are their role models? Find them.

Ok now I hear you say, "But the trainer is an expert in their field with loads of experience he/she can share with us! And a good trainer will get down to the level of attendees..." Really. So what if I was to grant my client's request and provide a one-day training program on Innovation? Let's see how this scenario typically plays out.

I, the know-it-all trainer am an "expert" on Innovation. I come into an organisation that I know relatively little about, let alone who the people in the room are in all their glory. I feel okay about that because I'm only in and out for the day. Quick introductions after I gloat over my extensive profile and glittering client list. I then pass out a course pack with the latest knowledge on innovation and its techniques.

I go through 6 modules, where I spend more than half the time on the first 2, then rush through the next 4 without many questions being answered if I even get any. I use all the engagement tricks in the book (I call them time-wasters) – deliver perfectly rehearsed ice-breakers, walk around the room, put people on the spot and test if they're listening, play YouTube videos, round up attendees into teams for some game play, crack some funnies, and do some stretching and clapping to save them from post-lunch slumber. You get the picture.

What's wrong with this picture? Everything. The "expert" does not know who he is teaching. His biggest concern is to spew out all the information in the time allotted. He wants to get a glaring recommendation so he makes it fun with time-wasters. And all in all he wants to get outta there in a jiffy with no compulsions to evaluate success or follow-up.

"But maybe the information provided was useful?" you might ask. The information is pre-packaged with no consideration of what's happening in terms of current performance. The course material feels pretty and branded but the exercises are not even remotely challenging (and very searchable on the internet). And there is absolutely nothing that attendees take away in terms of what they might apply back to their daily job.

Nor do they leave with an inspired will or motivation to act or an I-feel-good emotion. In fact, 9 out of 10 training program attendees whether in-house or through an external provider want to get out in a jiffy just like their expert trainer. I've seen it all too often. You don't have to guess what the first thing to get cut is when a company faces budget issues. And for good reasons too.

The point is I still get optimistic HR Managers or Department Heads or CEOs putting up an argument, "So what if there are bad trainers, fake experts and off-the-wall training programs out there. They're not all like that! Besides, it's the only way we know how to hope for change in our people. Otherwise they just keep doing whatever it is they are doing with no improvements. How else do we keep people engaged, excited, excelling and learning?"

Certainly not with the common practice of today, i.e. orthodox, lackluster, internet-searchable information that tells the employee to follow one-way or the highway.

3

The Days of Cascading are Numbered

I hope I've convinced you on some level that traditional training has not worked in a long while, and that businesses need a new paradigm. A new paradigm should allow human capital to take the learning and apply it directly onto their jobs with the passion and enthusiasm that employers go on about in their media bites. Many training courses and programs claim to do this, but I'm sorry, the ground reality speaks otherwise.

And they continue, "My dear, what you're talking about only applies to external training vendors with structured courses and public seminars. We do a lot of in-house training and the content is always relevant to our business. And the information is always based on what's cascaded right from the top." Nice try but this is far from enough to get your people engaged, excited and excelling.

Whether in-house or out-of-house, the results of most training programs are the same. No learning other than the rote kind, no questioning, no innovation, and short-term application at the most. Before you know it, you'll be sending the team on another booster course to force them into action. Is that what organisations should be aiming for? Of course not. "Of course we aim higher. Our aim with training is always to make a difference in the performance of employees." Right. And how's that working out for you?

How does your organisation / department / team evaluate whether the training program positively affects job performance? Most organisations stop at attendee feedback where employees are expected to give their honest opinion of the value of the administered course.

One will find a positive skew around "yes it was rather fun attending." But what about what was learned? Are they motivated to use the learning back at work? "Great speaker, great food, great setup, great structure, great time!" In fact, transfer of training onto the original work environment rarely occurs statistically speaking.

When I interview the same attendees privately and get into their heart of hearts, I usually get responses like: "We get sent to these things because HR has to show their mettle" or "The material was blatantly irrelevant for our niche" or "I don't trust this and sure wouldn't go try all this out tomorrow" or "Training here's a joke. It's good fun, but nothing more." The best comment I've heard is, "I have mastered the exquisite art of sleeping with my eyes open."

Anyhow, back to the contention that training is a way to get change in employee performance, supported by a cascaded strategy from the top... I've got news for everyone. The days of cascading are numbered. Training based on what needs to be cascaded down to the lower rungs of the corporate ladder is usually "customized".

"See! Isn't that a good thing?" Not really. Customization based on cascaded corporate strategies is, but naturally, considered legitimate by most organisations of today. As you might've gathered by now, I've set out to dethrone this common practice.

Cascading leads to at least 3 detriments. Chinese whispers, a loss in translation and most profane of all, no buy-in. In the Middle East where I reside and I'm sure elsewhere, business has been about the vision of a few leaders at the top and this tradition largely continues today. The image of one leader and many followers still endures in the hearts and minds of the people in many parts of the world.

But what would you predict if the strategies of a privileged few at the top were not entirely sustainable for the environment, the market, or for the new customer experience you're building? You'd have competitors that will take your place, customers who will disconnect from your brand and a significant loss in your best talent, not to mention a disengaged workforce.

A client once told me, "These people down there are in the 'untrainable' category. They refuse to learn and develop." On further investigation, most of them came to work everyday thinking, "We get told from the higher ups what to do anyway. Everything's cascaded from the top, so what's there to learn? All we have to do is do. We get paid for not thinking." I definitely agree. They refuse to develop if dumbed down.

I said earlier that companies may well need to resort to some training, e.g. for products and services that your people need to be experts in and sell to customers. But why don't we revisit this notion too? Here's a story I'd like to share from one of my clients back in 2008.

HR's chief complaint was that their product training had been ineffective guessing by the inability of salespeople to adequately answer customer queries from their last mystery shop campaign. "Can you design a better training program for us? My CEO expects our salespeople to answer customer questions!" Sigh. I can, but you know what? It would never work. And the lovely HR lady was ready to invest in something with no guaranteed results.

I turned her thinking around by suggesting an alternative paradigm. "Why don't you round up all your salespeople into focus groups and give them the role of your ideal customer. Now, let your CEO be the salesperson and answer their product-related questions. Then, just sit back and watch what happens. Update me with your results next week?"

Several things happened. 1) The CEO became aware of what the toughest questions were that his sales force faced on site - he realized that customer questions were no longer the same as when he first developed the product 2) The sales team lit up with amazing ideas to improve the product 3) A root cause was uncovered - one of the reasons the sales team were "not answering customer questions adequately" was because as per policy, they were randomly pocket searched by store managers in the middle of the day. This created huge mistrust and a direct lack of customer service 4) The sales process, which was part of the internal training program for many years, got scrapped and a new one reinvented together with the CEO right there in the room addressing critical points in daily customer interactions.

This famous retail giant has since reduced its investment in training and has made it HR's mandate to develop feedback systems throughout their business. This simple case study illustrates the power of learning from within, without structured material or an expert. The client and his/her team are always the experts every single time for every single goal.

If your organisation is one of many if not most, that does not actively involve its workforce in assessing top strategies, you are most likely foregoing one of the most efficient management styles for business success. Think about this - What if you spent your time developing feedback mechanisms instead of investing in the next big training program? Not only are you guaranteed better business strategies and therefore results, you are creating learning and development from within.

Before I forget, there were of course permanent key outcomes from this client, and many others who are now opening up, that need mention – engagement, communication, trust, brand excitement and better sales are now consistently observed results coming out of feedback systems, without having had any financial investment to begin with. So the next time you are looking at a new training course, ask yourself if your internal experts might do better in a forum, which surfaces tough work situations that actually happen. Training might be safe but it's also very sorry.

If you are CEO or the Head of your company, think of the organisational asset you would have simply by eliminating the "Roll it out!" cascading model. With feedback systems installed, people would buy in to the strategies you want executed, and you will cultivate your human capital to think as one unit. No more confused messages, no more resentment from down below or less of it, and no more robotic stimulus-response conditioning to maintain the illusion of a smooth sailing operation.

"Can you apply a feedback system to new employees who might still need the top-down lecture-style content-filled training?" Of course! And, what a better way than to turn them onto their jobs right from the get go. Can you imagine this scene – a group of new employees sitting through an orientation session that has them totally lost a few minutes in. Now replace it with the following scene.

A group of new employees comes in expecting a lecture on the history of the company. But what they get is an auditorium filled with their colleagues and managers egging them on to get on a podium. They are asked to speak about why they came here, and what they want the future of their new company to be. "Where will your unique abilities take us?!" New joiners are the ones orienting the old timers. The mold readily adjusts to new cookies coming in. Employees never forget their first day at work.

By the way, if you need to orient new employees about the history of your company, your company values, its mission, vision and product lines, you've either gone amiss with your selection process or you haven't done justice to your corporate brand. Just saying.

My message is simple. Most top-down cascaded strategic messages end up lost and unlived. Plus, there is by and large no value placed on assessing executioner buy-in. These strategic messages will as a result not effectively reach or convert target customers the way they should. As organisations run on this modus operandi, they are closing themselves off to untapped potential, markets, alliances, and communities.

These times call for transformational processes that are faster, more cost-effective, and result in deeper paradigm shifts. This needs to enable organisations to truly capture what they deserve at the lightening speed the market moves at. And that means facilitating strategic decisions by involving all effectible levels.

Cascading does the opposite. It dictates rather than facilitates. It hammers rather than enamors. It deflates rather than relates. It deals rather than heals.

I know what some of you might be thinking, "How on earth do I NOT cascade? We'd like to maintain the chain of command. And besides, there's way too many of us here. Any change we try to make has to be done in bits in small groups by the managers in charge. That's just the nature of change. It's slow, painful and people don't want it. So cascading is the only way."

No it isn't the only way. The reason I say this lies in our assumptions about how change happens. Why do so many leaders I talk to assume that change is this big scary monster achievable only with loads of disposable time and money?

Let's look at how change is managed in most organisations today and put it to the test.

Change Does Not Have to be Slow, Painful or Hard

I have to make a confession. Change management gurus and I are perpetually at loggerheads. In my brutally honest perspective, the change management profession has disintegrated into nothing more than project management, with a heavy emphasis on training. It's probably why training enjoys such empty popularity because it has overtones of being the primary tool for fostering change.

I cringe when I receive emails about the next change management certification course. "You can now be a certified Change Manager." What?! Besides being frightfully expensive all they really teach is the step-by-step project implementation process that is built from the cascading model. Change is more than just implementing a step-by-step project. And training people on how to manage projects is not how you deliver change.

I'd like to dispel some key assumptions made by change management. First off, change and management are two words that register as a classic oxymoron. You shouldn't have to manage change. Change is actually a natural order of things, be it how we evolve, how we think, what we perceive as a society, how we manage life and even our body cells die off every second to renew our self. You never step into the same river twice (thank you Heraclitus). Big change has never been forced.

Corporations still pay lip service to adapting to change. But they in fact enforce internal policies, strategies and procedures in a way that creates complacency and eventually hard resistance. And nobody in the organisation realizes how set in stone that resistance becomes. It is considered good behavior until of course the market begins to crash.

Demands from the market and the business environment force companies into changing heavily and slowly. And this kind of change is usually a very traumatic affair. It's no wonder that training gets high priority during these so-called change initiatives. Training has been the safest way to introduce the workforce to changing market demands and newer customer needs.

But being safe means low risk and low risk brings organisations back to square one. Square one is where the organisation keeps returning to time and again. It's a place that does not allow it to move forward. In other words square one ensures that no paradigm shifts or leaps in performance occur. Change is hence not imminent and the status quo of complacency remains.

As an organisation keeps returning to square one after failed training, it sets yet another stone on the wall of resistance. One of my colleagues in the training industry tried to catch me out by objecting, "Oh but what you are on about is just bad training. I mean if you don't have measures in place that monitor outcomes, of course training is ineffective. Anyone can tel you that." He was right but only halfway.

Tracking the outcomes of training is an obvous must-do. But how many organisations do it? And when they do so, the trackers aren't set up properly. And if the tracking measures happen to be set up right, they usually show no or low resu ts. Even if they do show results most are expressed as amateur percentages with no experimental research study as a backdrop or testing for statistical significance. Results are hard to attribute to the training program in many cases. Back to square one.

Back to square one for the umpteenth time, the Training Manager is now accountable for creating even more advanced level training - "Sales 10.5!". Additional bells and whistles that entail excessive monetary investment get included just to get the smallest changes in results.

For example, one such trick is to bring in a motivational speaker to excite the crowd. Just like a rock concert. Cnly the crowd isn't exactly full of raving fans. They might get momentary stress relief or break from the mundane. But a significart and sustainable change in performance on the job is beyond the scope of a popular motivational guru.

"Hey, if we can record a slight shift in the KFI meter, we'll take it!" Celebrating small wins is fine in my book but don't make it a habit that gets you stuck on small wins forever. It is always a let down when I see companies willing to deem mediocre increases as actual achievement.

I'm building up this experiential evidence to argue against the common thread between training and change management. They are a great match but their romance has been disastrous for business. Numerous research points out that up to 70% of organisational change management initiatives fail. Similarly, the ROI for training has been questionable.

As an Organisation Development practitioner for well over the last decade, here's 5 reasons I've found responsible for the alarming failure rate of training programs and change management projects: 1. They rely on so-called validated assessment tools. 2. Programs are planned and forced upon people without much choice in the matter. 3. Solutions, answers and decisions come from a select few in authority. 4. Too often, the impact is never felt organisation-wide. 5. Training and change management focus on measuring incremental change.

Let's take a close look at each of my cited reasons for failure, and the myths the industry uses as bait.

Myth #1. *The validated assessment tool.* People are the most variable subjects on earth. Most assessments tools yield different results at different times. For tools to be valid, results must be consistently reliable and they're just not. How can they stay valid when people's mindsets adapt in response to their experience all the time?

Tools such as psychometric and personality testing, which are so often used to label and determine the 'baseline' of an employee's abilities, are highly unreliable and inflatable. You are not the person you were.

Change management also uses diagnostic tools. These focus on diagnosing problems and solving them as they arise, which means one problem-solving project after another. Nothing more than the quality circle movement of the 80s. We're not in the 80s.

Many pre-training assessment tools try to establish a scientific baseline for individuals who are then put through training to "fix the gaps". Pre-testing is definitely the right way to go if you are recruiting for the military. Subjects here do not have much choice other than following orders. But in a world-class company employee choice is where competitive gains are to be made. This gets into my next point.

Myth #2. *The workforce has to undergo constant training and is required to change.* It's interesting when leaders tell me that their people must change. Ironically, their systems and culture make change so difficult and painful. Most training and change initiatives are forcibly administered on employees with no sense of choice, feedback or buy in. "You must change to our new system next week. It's your job!" Right. Ok.

It's interesting to note that a synonym of the word 'cascade' is 'force'. In the previous chapter, I talk about why cascading is futile. An example is how many of my clients show me elaborately cascaded top-down communication campaigns aiming to get people on board. However, the messaging on planned changes and new strategies boils down to this: "This is what's gonna happen. Like it or not. Don't like it? Get another job." How is that doing anything to engage your internal stakeholders?

Another client approached me once their ERP system was successfully installed and staff training completed. "There must be a reason why you've called me in Mr. B." I asked. His response, "I took all the training and project management my software vendor offered. But my people refuse to use it! They want to go back to Excel. I'm facing a mutiny." Mr. B had unknowingly built the great wall of resistance. This is an all too familiar outcome when change is unnaturally forced by a select few.

Myth #3. *The top tier knows best about what is to be done.* I do advocate that it is top management's job to steer the direction for the best interest of the business. However, that great wall of resistance is bolstered when decisions are made in pure isolation. This is another unmitigated feature of the cascading model. Top decisions are rolled out and forced down the throat of those who've got to execute it on the ground. And I can't tell you how many of those I've interviewed go, "If he thinks this new policy will fly with the customers I service day in and day out, he's nuts."

"So what? We have an organisation to run and al its members must do what they are paid to do." Sounds like a fair enough point. All I'm saying is people do their job much better when they support their top tier. Don't you pay your people to do exactly that? Support you in achieving your company's big goals? Let's get a grip on what "support" is.

Ask whether your human capital buys in to where you are steering your business, and them. Genuine support is what you want because that's energetically, resourcefully, motivationally and financially most effective. Google it. Cr better yet, ask Google.

I know you're already asking the million-dollar question like Mr. B did. "So. How do I get genuine support for this new system we spent over a million dollars on?" If you knew the answer, what would it be?

Myth #4. *Change and training should be done in small doses with small groups.* I do understand why a lot of leaders want to think this works best. Managing large numbers of people or very complex changes seems to be such a daunting endeavor.

But again, I take a different stand on this practice. If you work to change in small groups, the organisation's parts do not get aligned together. Small groups are usually trained in isolation. When this happens in my experience I notice a waste in time and resources. How so? In small groups, change must be constantly reinforced for it to stick. Why? Because the impact hasn't been adopted by the rest of the organisation.

For instance, say your procurement department undergoes re-training due to new purchasing guidelines cascaded (of course) from top management. They now need to buy alternative products from new suppliers, which the sales team must stock and sell. Resistance by your Sales team ensues as they are nonchalantly informed via a 1-page memo.

Even though a new procedure might prove temporarily beneficial, I've witnessed far too many departmental disharmonies resulting from change activities conducted one section at a time. "Why were we not told of your intention to do this!" or "We are the heart of this business. Can you explain why our input was deemed unnecessary?" are common flare-ups.

Which section / group / team would you say is the heart of your business? In my years of both qualitative and quantitative data gathering, every department believes they are the heart of the business. Yes it is their pride talking, but they would also be correct. So why do we insist on small group change and training when the heart extends much further?

I believe we've reached an era in business that demands a superior way of delivering change. One that accounts for how every subgroup of an organisation is impacted in real time. One that creates such a powerful simultaneous shift for all, that it would altogether reduce the need to continually monitor and measure.

Myth #5. *If you can't measure it, you can't manage it.* This is the point at which I get into a lot of hot water with my colleagues. I spoke earlier about how training spend is justified in order to show evidence of the smallest of positive results. I mean it when I say organisations are wasting precious resources when they meticulously measure. Huh?!

Keep calm and consider another possibility. Continuous improvement is not good enough. Why not? Because. Your customers don't have the luxury of waiting for you to improve at your leisurely rate. Feeling great about a 1% improvement has done nothing to change your profitability, cost-effectiveness or customer loyalty.

All the measurement systems in the world will not transform your business. Why? I am a star witness to many companies with incredible measurement, data and reporting tools. "We watch our numbers and track everything we do very closely." They want the numbers to change, but nothing else. They might as well be saying, "We wait at our slot machines everyday and hope for a windfall".

Numbers control businesses way too much and much too superfluously. Numbers on a dashboard are lifeless without the stories that got them on there. "Sure, that's obvious". Is it? Then why do so many organisations have "making money" as their only goal? Most businesses look at an end number for profitability, but forego the never-ending story of sustainability.

Big leaps, rather than small improvements, make stories of sustainability stick. Big leaps mean paradigm shifts where an organisation moves to a place of no return. Use this hack and you can never go back. So what's the hack? Divest in training and invest in transformation. And when do you know you have transformation?

When change is dramatically significant, measures play a supporting role rather than the lead role. Once there is a transformative shift, every activity, task, idea, plan or action becomes a reflection of a new culture. The change is so profound that measuring incremental improvements becomes a thing of the past. Gun for big change, not small amendments.

Measuring has become nothing more than an addiction that leads to analysis paralysis and ends up in data denial. I see leaders time and again come to me with large numerical spreadsheets, attempting to explain why their numbers can't possibly be true. "We got the best service award last year, so these complaint numbers can't be right." Or "Yes our engagement scores are pretty high. But we lost 5 of our top performers to the competition last month." The irony of it all.

Is it really about tracking whether 90% of the company is going okay? Maybe the focus should be on the 10% that gets you real exponential growth. The 90% then sorts itself out because of the overwhelming success of the 10% or it meets its end. Leaders and Managers know where and when the numbers are low. But they don't know why or how. And if they do, they go back to training for itsy bitsy increments that keep them glued to square one.

"But we gotta track everything to make sure things are running on time and with the right process." Fair enough. But what really creates growth, development, change and exponentia results? It's more than a numbers game. Development has to be so dramatic that it is seen, heard, echoed and felt without the need for measuring tools.

I once asked a business leader what his idea of a good investment is. His wise response: "The best investment is where the returns are infinite." Why focus on the finite, when possbilities are infinite?

Finite measurement is no longer the holy grail cf management. I'm asking you to make your numbers the result of a far greater story. The hallmark of which is a faster, deeper and investment-conscious system that manages itself.

A process so intuitive, natural and evolving that your organisation does not go back to its previous state. Change so dynamic that it captures market opportunities at the speed of need. A methodology that completely de-prioritizes cascading, training, measuring, experts and tools. A world far away from square one, where breakthrough shifts cannot not happen.

Come on over.

The **SPEED**Change™ Project

If you're still with me, I thank you. I've tried to summarize my experience with training and managing change in a short space. With the limitations I gathered, I've tried and tested alternative methods over the years. These methods have now culminated into a project I'm very excited to tell you about and I call it The **SPEED**Change™ Project.

The roots of **SPEED**Change™ come from the whole-systems movement pioneered by Kathleen Dannemiller in the 1960s. Roland Sullivan, who writes the foreword for this book, introduced the concept to me in 2004. One of the features of whole-systems is large-group interventions where as many as 500 to 1000 people come together in interactive events to transform their organisation.

With **SPEED**Change™, I'm adapting whole-systems for the Middle East and elsewhere. Many leaders still don't see beyond training and change management. Company cultures in this part of the world do not accept feedback from lower ends of the structure. High power distance and hierarchy prevail, and regimented training is used to enforce tasks. Distilled remains of HR's military history are still alive. Phrases like "chain of command" and job titles with "Officer" still exist in workplaces here.

Even though the whole-systems process has a series of milestones before the big group events, getting an entire organisation together with top leadership is still taboo around here. And allowing people the power to express flaws to their CEO? Even anonymously, that's a bigger taboo.

I do understand these concerns. Whole-systems thinking comes across too traumatic and unrealistic for traditional companies. "Getting the entire company in one room and steering the ship together? Sounds crazy and expensive and way too confrontational." The traditional company also hangs on to what outside experts have to say. Shaking off that value will shake the core of organisational cultures all over the region.

But I do believe whole-systems is the future. Entities that want the world as their oyster, not just their local market, will seek superior change systems. And I intend to be the Change Agent in that global wave. I designed **SPEED**Change™ inspired by the stories of a few organisations that have used whole-systems elements in one form or another.

The **SPEED**Change™ Project is my answer to training. Its essence combines a feedback system with involved learning that focuses on on-the-job action. The underlying philosophy eliminates the outside expert, speaker and trainer. It gets the expertise from the organisation itself where it always was. And as the name suggests, it goes deeper in to get faster change.

The Project is all of 1 week around 1 Topic of Priority with 3 internal members. Then the process and elements are applied on a core team of 8 participants. A traditional organisation is able to handle this scale.

Here are the key elements of The **SPEED**Change™ Project.

Element #1. *The Problem is Not the Issue.* The orientation moves away from solving a problem. Problem solving is not the goal of this Project. It's only a by-product of this experience.

The first piece of business is called an Aspiration Session. The **SPEED**Change™ Agent helps settle on a Topic of Priority (TOP) with the CEO or the owner of that topic (TOP Owner). The topic is not chosen because it is a chronic problem. It is chosen because it has the potential to take the team to new frontiers. The conversation is deep and can get emotional because the CEO must transform and align himself first.

The CEO / TOP Owner uncovers his aspirations for the core team. He is wowed at the possibilities beyond finite numbers. He knows that transformation is the only way forward, where the team must never go back to its current state. He wants to say, "Good riddance to square one!"

An Aspiration Session is not only about choosing a topic and setting the tone for change. The real work is in selecting who the participants are and how they're going to execute the Topic of

Priority. "Who should I choose to go through this process? Who are the champions questioning the current state? Who are the ones that need to let go of resistance?"

The CEO is guided to form key questions for the TOP that need to be answered by his team only. The answers are always actionable and transformative in nature. The questions never focus on a problem to be solved. They are designed to elicit perspectives from all subgroups. This questionnaire tool is used in one-to-one interviews with the core team.

The final discussion point in the Aspiration Session is the development of a simple but effective reward scheme. What does the team look forward to once business results have broken through? The CEO must reward the team as a whole for taking that leap of faith out of square one.

At this point, the Agent has served as a catalyst to transforming the CEO / TOP Owner. She has got him aligned to the infinite possibilities that will be fulfilled when his team also transforms. She has enabled the CEO / TOP Owner to let go and begin to trust his team. A new perspective on leadership has given him a new set of core beliefs.

This shift wouldn't have happened if the Agent wasn't who she was.

Element #2. *Out with the Trainer and in with the* **SPEED**Change™ *Agent.* There is no expert instructing or training. Agents are the only external set of people on site (if there aren't any internally qualified). So who is the Agent and what is their role?

The Agent is the primary facilitator of the Project. She drives every element of The **SPEED**Change™ Project. Her main objective is to support the CEO's aspirations around the Topic of Priority. And she is responsible for how the **SPEED**Change™ process flows.

Agents are qualified in the competencies of transformative change. In my experience, these competencies are not so much about skill. If who they are as a person meets the mark, skills are pretty much pre-developed.

The first competency I look for is whether an Agent is philosophically inclined. Do they ask the big questions about existence? What is their personal transformation story? Are they black and white when it comes to ethics? Have they been raised with dogmatic mental schemas? What is their view of what a human being is? What does consciousness mean for them? Do they have political convictions? What makes them angry? These questions are very much a part of my work every day.

You will find that the Agents I'm talking about are not your typical corporate trainers. When I get approached by trainers to collaborate on "change projects" (write plans and execute them), I ask what their philosophies of learning and change are. Whenever I've brought up any of the questions above, I get this kind of response: "What's that got to do with the client requirement?" Select your Change Agent carefully.

As an Agent of Change I insist on certain practices. Agents have no hidden agenda other than supporting CEO aspirations. They practice non-judgment, allow every participant their space and voice, and are credited with creating a safe environment for key questions to surface. They take a long look at cultural dynamics and build trust with every stakeholder. They care deeply about an organisation's destiny, and are vulnerably open to being transformed themselves. They are essentially the tool.

In practical terms, the Agent does not speak for more than 10 minutes. She does not offer advice or tell the group what to do. She is not an expert in the organisation's industry or products and neither does she need to be. She comes armed with the CEO's aspirations and the trust built with individual participants. She asks questions, guides dialogue, facilitates feedback systems and documents verbal data.

It is a rewarding role. Not only for personal fulfillment. Many internal Agents in my network around the globe often update me with news of getting promoted or offers of profit share. They are seen as heroes. They provide the engine for the organisation's train of greatness.

Element #3. *A Design Team etches the dream.* The Design team is where the magic happens. This is a team of 3 champions who are the strongest allies for team transformation. They might not all agree and have varied opinions, but they have a common unifier – the desire to be better and to challenge the current state.

The Agent has helped the CEO to select this dream team. They are crucial in the team's paradigm shift. What are the features that make the Design Team work best? Besides having a common dream of being better? The 3 champions are preferred to represent different levels, sport conflicting opinions, unique perspectives and have no fear to express. This is ideal.

No they do not have to be senior level only. No they do not need to have 100 years of experience under their belt. No they do not have to be high performers. And no they do not have to like the CEO.

The Design Team get together with the Agent. They co-create the most exciting, dynamic, transformative one-day meeting agenda for their team. This is not about planning a corporate event with games, speakers or entertainment. This is about designing conversations, learning activities, creative thinking exercises based on the Topic of Priority. Each activity in the agenda is fine-tuned by the Agent in this design meeting.

The Design Team is the Agent's consultant. The Design Team knows what the culture, politics and current situation of the environment is. They know what activities will work best because of who is in the room. They get to pick who sits next to who and who gets paired up with who.

The Agent's duty is to assist the Design Team with determining features of each activity that would enhance their effectiveness. She also assists in developing pre-activity formats and establishing content for learning objectives. "You mean training program content?" Ha, no.

One of they key aspects of the Design Team is that they create content from true stories. For e.g. I've assisted one of my client's Design Teams to develop a critical incident bank. It documented key occurrences in a business situation that warranted learning and lessons to be observed. The bank was used as part of a scenario exercise.

In fact, this is one criterion I insist on when helping CEOs choose their Topic of Priority. I ask, "Do you have plenty of stories in your company that illustrate the importance of this topic?" If stories aren't there, they will have some form of data that speaks about it. Like expertise, content is also sourced and harnessed right from within the organisation.

Content also comes from an interview data report compiled by the Agent. Before collaborating with the Design Team, she has already interviewed all 8 team members in confidential one-on-one sessions. I have not covered the details of this, but these interviews are an essential feature of The **SPEED**Change™ Project. It gets into each individual's feelings and desires around the Topic of Priority. She builds trust with every one of them, knows their motivations, and makes them count in the process.

The Design Team don't come out of the room until they get the agenda right. We've had instances where they went on for a full day and at other times, a few hours. This one-day transformative agenda is a tool that's internally built to initiate team transformation. It is valid because it is meant for this team, in this organisation, for this time. It's a far cry from training programs that are one size fits all for any and all entities.

Element #4. *The Smartest Person in the Room is the Room.* The one-day transformative meeting arrives. The Agent's duty is to ensure that facilities are set up properly for all activities. She adheres to the ground rules set by the Design Team and acts as a guardrail to execute the agenda. Her skill also comes into play when the agenda has to be modified on the spot in cases of participants expressing reservations or fear. She also is a timekeeper and formally documents all ideas and decisions that transpire.

Because the Agent knows all members of the team, the battle is half won. The group enters the room already excited about the new synergy that's about to emanate. They know what conversations are about to take place. They know its going to be an emotional day but there are no surprises. The resistance level has dropped because a neutral party has heard them individually in person about the subject at hand. Happens every time.

This transformative meeting focuses on the whole system. This means that everyone affected by the Topic of Priority is involved in shaping its future. Everyone is equal with their own truths. The activities and conversations are organized in such a way that input from all is gathered safely. The Agent analyses in real time, what the room is saying and learning. The elephant in the room is the room itself.

The **SPEED**Change™ Agent assures the CEO of three deliverables:

1. *A Change Blueprint for the team.* This incorporates the results from learning activities. What has the team learned about the TOP? What were the contributing factors to align the team? The transformative meeting not only reveals new goals that all the members agree to. The "coming to agreement" process is such that a newfound respect for fellow team members emerges.

2. *Individual Application Plans.* Created by the individual team members themselves, they outline on-the-job actions with timelines. Applying the learning back on to the job is guaranteed because people support what they create. The rewards are in it for the team once there is a paradigm shift. The CEO will see that this team has left square one for good.

3. *Accountability Feedback System.* The Change Blueprint and Individual Application Plans go through a formal feedback system. The Design Team is assigned responsibilities of follow-up and implementation support to pull the team toward its new vision. An online communication platform is created. Team members and the CEO / TOP Owner are aware of progress. Rewards set by the CEO are broadcasted once business results are evident.

So when would The **SPEED**Change™ Project not work? Learning, change and transformation will not occur if any of the following factors is present.

1. *The CEO is not in it.* The idea of "change in a week" sounds like a quick fix to many potential clients. Once the primary client is identified, the Agent assesses him. With her skill she will be able to discern whether the CEO is willing and able to transform first.

   The team he is in charge of will not apply new learning back on the job if he does not commit to change along with them. If the CEO or TOP Owner expects breakthrough business results and a new culture from his team, the Agent ensures that he's in it for real. In cases where this is not so, it is the fiduciary duty of the **SPEED**Change™ Agent to deny service.

2. *The participants selected for the Project do not fit.* The selection of participants in the Project can make or break it. The Topic of Priority (TOP) must involve all who are directly affected by it. If the TOP is "Increase in Sales" then the obvious choice is your core sales team.

   If your TOP is something like "Succession Planning" or "Trust" then it might be that specific people from various sections are chosen to go through the Project. This selection process is key. If anyone affected is left out of this experience, we haven't accounted for the "whole".

   A **SPEED**Change™ Agent's duty is to thoroughly investigate with the CEO who the right participants for the Design Team and core team are. The ideal number for a core team is 8. If there are potentially more participants, the Agent expands the Project accordingly.

3. *The trust level is below zero for a TOP.* Selecting the Topic of Priority is as important as selecting participants. Sometimes CEOs will get ahead of themselves and choose topics that their team is not ready for.

Traditional organisations may have excessively toxic work cultures. The level of trust between the CEO / TOP Owner and the team could be too low to withstand a dynamically charged week long process. The politics is too heavy to question the status quo in unity. In such a case, the Agent must design a Topic Of Priority that first and foremost heals and unifies the team with the CEO.

The Agent must coach with the CEO to iron out these 3 factors jointly for The **SPEED**Change™ Project to be on course.

The real benefits of **SPEED**Change™ are about what happens apart from business clarity. Communication, transparency, trust, engagement and fairness evolve naturally. Change is profound and can be seen without measurement. Business breakthroughs and individual learning do not have to be meticulously managed after a transformative leap. Change is always a natural progression.

A 5th century Chinese philosopher named Lao-Tse said it best.

"If you tell me, I will hear. If you show me, I will see.
But if you let me experience, I will learn."

6

The Future of Change

My dream is to see The **SPEED**Change™ Project evolve into Whole-Systems change for entire organisations, not just one team, in my part of the globe. To see 1000 or more people come together in transformative events, with Design Teams creating history and shaping futures.

It is proven. A case from the U.S.A. documented this statement, "People of all levels went out to speak about what was done. It had an impact on the way that we did our work. Instantly we started to see change in the attitudes of our employees and how that affected customers. The results told us we were unleashing magic." - Allstate Insurance Agent.

And in South Africa, "I have just seen the most powerful transformational experience ever in our country." - Minister in the South African Government, after witnessing ABSA Bank's transformative event. ABSA became the most loved brand in South Africa leaving Coca Cola at #2.

It's a matter of time before companies in the Middle East and other parts of the world echo these statements.

I'd like to make a few predictions about how change will be perceived and managed. Organisations are already frustrated with the ineffectiveness of training to influence change. I believe training is going out the door. It will make way for superior systems to deliver organisation-wide change, team learning and individual development. Here's what I see happening:

Future #1. *Large Group Dynamics and Collaborative Environments.* Big change happens naturally when the entire system steers the ship together. Not one person at a time or separate groups at separate times. Large group dynamics will be utilized when organisations realize that paradigm shifts are not for the piecemeal-oriented. All global revolutions have been a testament to this.

Business will increasingly get collaborative instead of competitive. The competitive environment will no longer be sustainable (maybe not in my lifetime, but this is something I'm profoundly inclined to bet on).

Companies will simulate nature and mesh with other businesses in the environment. The boundaries of large conglomerates will blur with their acquisitions, partnerships and community links. Stress of competition will be replaced with growth-for-all in collaboration. The implications for whole-system interventions are obvious.

Future #2. *Consultant Role and Background Redefined.* The role of the Consultant will change. No more are they the experts in strategy. No more will they look at their clients' watches and dictate what time it is. Their knowledge base will primarily be the social interaction of the organisation's members with established processes, philosophies and culture. They make leaders believe that the expertise is within.

Existential Philosophers, Social Psychologists and Organizational Anthropologists will be in demand to manage large-group, system-wide interventions. They will have the ability to direct conflicting subcultures, subgroups and polarities as business boundaries start to get distorted. Millennials vs. old-school, creatives vs. task masters, technology vs. human minds are polarities that will be embraced as part of one system.

Future #3. *"Agility" the Only Competency.* The one and only competency an organisation will need is flexibility, speed and the ability to respond effectively. The organisation must be agile to respond to opportunities as they present themselves in real time. This is why cascading and planning will die. The world does not wait for 5-year strategic plans to materialize.

This core competency will be the mother of all measuring tools. Agility is the pinnacle of transformation that will be required for futuristic business practices. I chuckle inside when potential clients come to me and ask, "We need your help in developing our 5-year strategic plan." And I politely answer, "Your 5-year plan will be obsolete in 6 months the way your business environment is. Concentrate on developing an agile response system instead."

Future #4. *Culture Eats Strategy for Breakfast, Lunch and Dinner.* Organisations will have no choice but to create a business process culture of agility to continue their story of sustainability. This means the right people will make natural demands for a personal authority to act and independence in thought. They will demand their right as free agents to respond to business needs without red tape, a chain of command or paper pushing. They will mirror customer demands.

Talent will be drawn to organisations with an agility-centric culture, where a) a mistake is just another result b) agile risk offsets the fear of financial loss c) values propel all decisions d) employees are considered owners e) ideas and innovation are open source platforms. f) organisations have bigger reasons to exist, i.e. making money is not the primary goal. The future is already here in this sense with Gen Y and Gen Z.

Culture will outweigh strategy every time. Strategists will make way for Social Scientists. Why? You can buy all the strategy in the world but you cannot buy a culture. And if culture and mindset do not deliberately enable strategy to flow, no amount of investment will bring returns.

Future #5. *Less measurement. More Paradigm Shifts.* Big sustainability only wants to see big changes in results. The future holds no place for measuring incremental improvements because they do nothing to change the game. Measuring will be based on how well every person, process, system and product adheres to the mother competency of agility.

The agility of business is not limited to how fast, well or effectively the organisation responds to market needs. It is about being ahead of the game and anticipating the future with endless possibilities. Finite numbers will not cut it anymore. In an interview with Forbes, Steve Jobs said, "We do no market research. We don't hire consultants. We just want to make great products." A man ahead of his time.

Apple is a perfect example of a company living the future in the now. Their customers did not ask for an iPod. Apple's team thought about the possibility, and voila, the rest is history. Now, people "need" an iPod. Product development did not rely on what the numbers were saying. There were no numbers. Only possibilities, which couldn't be held back.

Future #6. *Less process. More Conversation.* More agility will mean reductions in rigid business processes. We will eventually bid adieu to the legacy of the lean system. It'll be a drain on resources to keep systems and processes updated and tested. Making sure systems are enforced and followed are already major headaches. People do not follow them to a T anyway. Discipline to follow specific instructions and orders is well on its way to erosion with our millennial generation.

The focus will move to conversations and on-the-spot collaborative technology platforms. It'll be easier to create and run conversation-based feedback protocols and temporary project teams. These are flexibly structured and change when markets require them to. Machines might still be in use. How products and their sales funnels are designed however will be contingent upon open, fluid, deep conversations.

Before I leave you to ponder if all this means anything for your business, here are my last thoughts (for now). What am I saying in the big scheme of things?

Cascading will be a thing of the past. Feedback from the whole system will be necessary to move forward. Organisations will master sustainability through agility-centric cultures. Change Agents will be groomed within companies to facilitate transformation in alliance with social scientists. Trainers passionate about paradigm shifts will go back to get Philosophy degrees. Positive Futurists will replace problem solvers. The Transformation Office will be a regulated department across businesses that survive into the future.

There you have it. The **SPEED**Change™ Project is my contribution to the business and community ecosystem the future is preparing us for. I am eager to join thinkers who share my perspective to create this future together. May teams, businesses, and communities the world over experience new paradigms and breakthroughs. May they awaken to the fact that they will never remain the same.

About The Author

After over a decade of excellence in advisory services all over the Middle East, Mubeena Mohammed rebranded her Company in 2014 to meet global demands for her expertise. As CEO of Scholar Consultants, the mission of her Company is to "build authentic connections between Management and their Human Capital".

Mubeena has personally provided HR and strategy advisory to high-profile global organisations including Abu Dhabi and Dubai Government entities, American multi-national companies, and large local family businesses in the UAE since 2003.

She was awarded a Bachelor of Arts (B.A.) degree in two majors (Psychology and Philosophy) in May 2001 from Hofstra University, New York with departmental honors in Psychology. She received her Master of Arts (M.A.) degree in Industrial/Organisational Psychology in May 2003 also from Hofstra University.

Her sporting interests include salsa dancing and she was a national swimmer back in the day. She received her 1st Dan Black Belt in Shotokan Karate in 2010. She also produces oil and acrylic paintings and studies spirituality when she makes downtime. She is currently working on her first fiction novel based on her business and philosophical studies. The **SPEED**Change™ Project is her first business book.

Corporate Sites:

ScholarConsultants.com

TransformingOrganisations.com

Book Sites:

SPEEDChangeProject.com

Social Media:

Facebook.com/ScholarConsultants

Google.com/+ScholarConsultants

LinkedIn.com/company/Scholar-Consultants

Twitter.com/HRConsultantUAE

Youtube.com/user/ScholarConsultants